The most popular girls names for 2023:

Aadhya

Aadi

Aadya

Aahana

Aaleyah

Aaliyah

Aamanda

Aamber

Aanya

Aaria

Aariel

Aarna

Aarohi

Aarya

Aasta

Aayla

Abai

Abarrane

Abbey

Abbie

Abbigail

Abby

Abbygail

Abélia

Abella

Abelle

Abercrombie

Aberdeen

Abhainn

Abigail

Abigale

Abmel

Abrial

Abriella

Abrielle

Abril	Addalyn
Abygail	Addelyn
Acacia	Addien
Acadia	Addilyn
Aceline	Addilynn
Ada	Addison
Adah	Addisyn
Adaira	Addyson
Adalee	Adela
Adalicia	Adelaid
Adalie	Adelaida
Adalina	Adelaide
Adalind	Adélaïde
Adaline	Adele
Adaliz	Adelia
Adaly	Adelie
Adalyn	Adelin
Adalyne	Adelina
Adalynn	Adeline
Adalynne	Adelisa
Adamaris	Adelise
Adara	Adeliza

The BIG Book of Girls Names 2023

By Jane Summers

Adelle	Aella
Adelyn	Aelwen
Adelyne	Aelwin
Adelynn	Aenya
Adelynne	Aeres
Aderyn	Aerfen
Adette	Aeris
Adhya	Aeron
Adilene	Aerona
Adina	Aeronwen
Adira	Aeronwy
Aditi	Aethwy
Adley	Afanen
Adora	Afon
Adrian	Afric
Adriana	Afrodille
Adrianna	Agate
Adriel	Agathe
Adrienne	Agnes
Advika	Ahana
Adwen	Aibhilin
Aednat	Aibhlin

Aibhlinn	Aillin
Aibhne	Ailsa
Aibreán	Ailyn
Aida	Aimee
Aidan	Aimeé
Aideen	Aimée
Aigéan	Aimil
Aila	Aindrea
Ailani	Áine
Ailany	Ainhoa
Ailbe	Ainslee
Ailbhe	Ainsley
Aileana	Ainslie
Ailee	Aira
Aileen	Airgid
Aileene	Airlia
Ailene	Airlie
Ailey	Aisha
Ailia	Aislin
Ailie	Aisling
Ailis	Aislinn
Ailish	Aislynn

Aitana	Alayna
Aithnea	Alba
Aiyana	Albane
Aiyanna	Albertine
Aiyleen	Aleah
Aiza	Aleanbh
Akira	Aledwen
Akshara	Aleeah
Alaa	Aleen
Alaia	Aleena
Alaina	Aleenah
Álainn	Aleia
Alaiya	Alejandra
Alana	Aleksandra
Alanah	Aleksandrina
Alani	Alena
Alanis	Alessa
Alanna	Alessandra
Alannah	Alessi
Alaya	Alessia
Alayah	Alex
Alayla	Alexa

Alexandra	Alijana
Alexandria	Alima
Alexandrine	Alina
Alexi	Alinah
Alexia	Alinna
Alexis	Alisa
Alexsus	Alisha
Alexus	Alison
Alexxa	Alissa
Aleyah	Alisson
Aleyda	Alivia
Aleyna	Aliya
Aleyza	Aliyah
Alezae	Aliyana
Alia	Aliza
Aliah	Alizae
Aliana	Alizah
Aliane	Alizay
Alianna	Alize
Alice	Alizeé
Alicia	Alizée
Alienor	Allana

Allayna	Aloyse
Allegra	Alsace
Allegro	Alsatia
Allemande	Althea
Allerie	Alva
Allete	Alwynne
Allie	Alya
Allison	Alyah
Allisson	Alyana
Allouette	Alyanna
Alloura	Alycia
Allura	Alyna
Allure	Alynna
Ally	Alyson
Allyson	Alyssa
Alma	Alysson
Alodie	Amabel
Alondra	Amaia
Alora	Amairani
Alouetta	Amairany
Alouette	Amal
Alowette	Amalia

Amalie	Ameera
Amanda	Amelia
Amande	Amelie
Amandeep	Amélie
Amandine	Ameline
Amani	America
Amara	Amerie
Amarah	Amérique
Amaranth	Ames
Amari	Amethyst
Amariah	Ami
Amarie	Amia
Amarine	Amiah
Amaris	Amie
Amaryllis	Amilia
Amaya	Amina
Amayah	Aminah
Ambar	Amira
Amber	Amirah
Amberly	Amiya
Ambre	Amiyah
Ambrette	Amor

Amora	Anaiya
Amore	Anaiyah
Amoretta	Analeah
Amorette	Analee
Amorra	Anali
Amour	Analia
Amoura	Analiah
Amoux	Analisa
Amser	Analise
Amy	Analiyah
Amya	Analy
An	Ananya
Ana	Anastasia
Anabel	Anaya
Anabella	Anayah
Anabelle	Ancelote
Anaelle	Anchoret
Anahi	Ancy
Anahit	Andi
Anais	Andie
Anaise	Andra
Anaisha	Andrea

Andrée	Anita
Anessa	Aniya
Angel	Aniyah
Angela	Anjali
Angéle	Ann
Angelette	Anna
Angelia	Annabal
Angelica	Annabel
Angelie	Annabell
Angelina	Annabella
Angeline	Annabelle
Angelique	Annabeth
Angélique	Annaleah
Angharad	Annalee
Angie	Annalia
Ani	Annalie
Ania	Annaliese
Anice	Annalisa
Anika	Annalise
Anisa	Annamarie
Anisha	Annbell
Anissa	Anne

Anne-marie

Annelise

Annette

Annick

Annie

Annika

Annique

Annot

Annwyl

Annwyll

Anny

Ansley

Anslie

Antinea

Antionette

Antoinette

Antonella

Antonia

Antonie

Antwahnette

Antwanetta

Antwinett

Anuhea

Anvi

Anvika

Anwen

Anwylle

Anwyn

Anya

Aoibhe

Aoibheann

Aoibhín

Aoibhinn

Aoibhneas

Aoife

Apolline

Apple

Appoline

Appolinia

April

Aquitaine

Ara

Arabella

Arabelle

Arabesque	Aria
Araceli	Ariadna
Aracely	Ariadne
Aramis	Ariah
Aranrhod	Ariana
Arantxa	Arianda
Arantza	Ariane
Aranza	Arianell
Araya	Arianna
Ardara	Arianne
Ardelle	Arianny
Arden	Arianrhod
Ardis	Arianwen
Ardiss	Arianwyn
Ardyce	Ariany
Ardys	Aribella
Ardyss	Arie
Areli	Arieana
Arelie	Ariel
Arely	Ariela
Argene	Ariella
Ari	Arielle

Arina	Arlo
Arionna	Arluene
Aris	Armande
Arisbeth	Armani
Ariya	Armantine
Ariyah	Armel
Arizbeth	Armelle
Arjane	Arriana
Arjean	Arrow
Arkansas	Artemis
Arlais	Artis
Arleen	Artois
Arlena	Arwen
Arlene	Arya
Arlet	Aryana
Arleta	Aryanna
Arleth	Aryonna
Arlett	Asceline
Arletta	Asees
Arlette	Asha
Arleyne	Ashanti
Arline	Ashauna

Ashelynn	Astin
Ashlee	Astra
Ashleen	Astrid
Ashleena	Atarah
Ashleigh	Athdara
Ashley	Athena
Ashlie	Atziri
Ashling	Aubergine
Ashlinne	Auberta
Ashly	Auberte
Ashlyn	Aubree
Ashlynn	Aubrey
Ashlynne	Aubri
Ashton	Aubriana
Asia	Aubrianna
Asiya	Aubrie
Asma	Aubriella
Aspen	Aubrielle
Aspyn	Aud
Asra	Auda
Assumpta	Aude
Asthore	Audra

Audree	Austine
Audrey	Austyn
Audriana	Autumn
Audrianna	Ava
Audrie	Avah
Audrina	Avalbane
August	Avalon
Aulani	Avalyn
Auld	Avalynn
Aura	Avani
Aure	Avayah
Aurèle	Aveline
Aurelia	Aven
Aurelie	Averi
Aurélie	Averie
Aurelle	Avery
Aurla	Avian
Aurora	Aviana
Aurore	Avianna
Aurorette	Avigail
Auryn	Avignon
Austin	Aviva

Avleen	Aynslee
Avneet	Ayra
Avni	Ayslin
Avon	Ayslyn
Avonlea	Ayva
Avril	Ayvah
Avyanna	Azalea
Awen	Azaria
Awena	Azariah
Axelle	Azélie
Aya	Azeneth
Ayah	Azucena
Ayana	Azul
Ayanna	Azure
Ayat	Babette
Ayda	Baby
Ayesha	Baie
Ayla	Bailee
Aylani	Bailey
Ayleen	Báisteach
Aylen	Baize
Aylin	Ballantine

Ballou	Beaumont
Bambi	Bebe
Banan	Bebhinn
Barbara	Bec
Bardot	Bechet
Baroness	Bechette
Barran	Becky
Barri	Bedeelia
Barry	Bedelia
Bastienne	Begonia
Bastina	Beibhinn
Baye	Beige
Baylee	Belcia
Beagan	Belen
Bealtaine	Belinah
Beara	Belinda
Beata	Beline
Beatrice	Belisse
Béatrice	Bella
Beatrix	Bellamy
Beatriz	Bellarose
Beau	Bellatrix

Belle	Bernedette
Bellette	Bernelle
Bellina	Bernice
Belvia	Bernyce
Benadette	Berry
Bénédicte	Berthe
Benilde	Bertille
Benoite	Bertrice
Bentley	Beryl
Beny	Beste
Berenice	Betania
Bérénice	Beth
Berenicia	Betha
Berkeley	Bethan
Berkley	Bethany
Berlin	Bethel
Bern	Bethwyn
Bernadette	Betrys
Bernadine	Betsy
Bernardene	Betty
Bernardine	Bevany
Berne	Beverly

Bevin	Blanca
Bexley	Blanchard
Bianca	Blanche
Bianka	Blanchefleur
Bibi	Bláth
Bibiane	Blathnaid
Bichette	Blathnat
Biddy	Blayke
Bidelia	Blaze
Bidella	Blessing
Bidon	Bleu
Bijou	Bleuzen
Bijoux	Blevine
Billie	Blodwedd
Bina	Blodwen
Birdie	Blodwyn
Blaine	Blodwynne
Blair	Blondelle
Blaire	Blossom
Blaise	Bluebell
Blake	Blythe
Blakely	Bo

Bobbi	Brady
Bobbie	Braelyn
Bonne	Braelynn
Bonnebell	Braith
Bonnee	Brana
Bonnell	Brandi
Bonney	Brandie
Bonni	Brandy
Bonnibel	Brangwen
Bonnibell	Branna
Bonnibelle	Branwen
Bonnie	Brauwin
Bonnie-Jo	Braylee
Bonnin	Brazil
Bonny	Brea
Bonny-Jean	Breana
Bonny-Lee	Breanna
Boudica	Breanne
Bouvier	Breckyn
Bowie	Breda
Bradee	Brede
Bradi	Bree

Breeann	Bridgette
Breeanna	Bridgit
Breeanne	Bridie
Breeda	Brie
Breehan	Brieanna
Breen	Briella
Breena	Brielle
Breezy	Brienna
Brenda	Brieon
Brenna	Brier
Brenne	Brigette
Bretta	Brighe
Bria	Brighid
Briallen	Brighton
Briana	Brigid
Brianna	Brigitte
Brianne	Briley
Briar	Brin
Bricen	Brinley
Brid	Brinn
Bride	Brinna
Bridget	Briona

Brisa	Bronwen
Briseida	Bronwin
Briseis	Bronwyn
Briseyda	Bronwynn
Brissa	Brooke
Bristol	Brooklyn
Britney	Brooklynn
Britta	Brownyn
Brittani	Brucina
Brittany	Brucine
Brittney	Brunette
Brody	Bryana
Brogan	Bryanna
Brogann	Bryce
Brogyn	Brylee
Bron	Bryn
Bronach	Bryna
Bronagh	Brynelle
Bronia	Brynlee
Bronnie	Brynleigh
Bronny	Brynn
Bronte	Brynna

Brynnan	Cadhla
Brynne	Cadi
Bryonna	Cadie
Bryony	Cady
Buddug	Cael
Bunni	Caela
Bunnie	Caelainn
Burgundy	Caelan
C'Ceal	Caeley
Cabernet	Caelyn
Cabriole	Caera
Cacee	Caerwyn
Cacelia	Cagney
Cachet	Cai
Caci	Caia
Cacia	Caihla
Cacie	Caila
Cacy	Cailean
Cadeau	Caileigh
Cadence	Cailie
Cadette	Cailyn
Cadewyn	Cain

Cainell

Caireann

Caisee

Caisey

Caisi

Caisie

Cait

Cáit

Caitir

Caitlin

Caitlyn

Caitrin

Caitrina

Caitriona

Caitríona

Calais

Calantha

Caleigh

Calgary

Cali

Calia

Calista

Caliste

Caliyah

Calla

Callan

Callen

Callie

Calliope

Callista

Calloway

Calynn

Cam

Camaran

Camari

Cambaria

Cambree

Cambria

Cambrie

Camden

Camdyn

Camellia

Cameran

Cameren

Cameri

Cameron

Cameryn

Camesha

Cameshia

Cami

Camila

Camilla

Camille

Campbell

Camrin

Camron

Camryn

Camrynn

Candace

Candice

Candide

Candy

Cantrelle

Caoilainn

Caoilfhionn

Caoilfinn

Caoilinn

Caoime

Caoimhe

Capri

Caprice

Capucine

Cara

Caraf

Caragh

Careshmeh

Caress

Caresse

Carey

Cari

Cariad

Carina

Caris

Carissa

Carla

Carlee

Carley

Carlie

Carlin

Carly

Carmela

Carmella

Carmen

Carol

Carolina

Caroline

Carolyn

Caron

Carressa

Carrey

Carrick

Carrie

Carrigan

Carroll

Carter

Cartier

Caru

Carwen

Carys

Caryse

Caryss

Carysse

Casadee

Casandra

Cascade

Cascáidigh

Cascy

Casee

Casey

Casi

Casidee

Casidy

Casie

Cassadee

Cassadi

Cassadie

Cassadina

Cassady

Cassandra

Casse

Casseday

Cassee

Cassey

Cassi

Cassia

Cassiddy

Cassidee

Cassidi

Cassidie

Cassidy

Cassie

Cassity

Cassye

Casy

Casye

Cataleya

Catalina

Cate

Caterina

Cathaleen

Cathaline

Catherine

Cathleen

Cathy

Catiana

Caton

Catreena

Catrin

Catrina

Catriona

Cattaleya

Cattleya

Catylyn

Caycee

Cayci

Caycie

Caydence

Cayenne

Cayla

Caylee

Cayleen

Cayleigh

Cayley

Caylia

Caylie

Cayse

Caysee	Cecilea
Caysey	Cecilee
Caysi	Ceciley
Caysie	Cecilia
Cazzee	Ceciliane
Cazzi	Cecilie
Cazzie	Cecilija
Ceallach	Cecilla
Ceara	Cecille
Cece	Cecillia
Ceceilia	Cecily
Ceceleah	Cecilyann
Ceceley	Ceclia
Ceceli	Cecyle
Cecelia	Cecylia
Cecely	Cecyliah
Cecelyn	Cee
Cecette	Céibhfhionn
Ceciel	Ceicelia
Cecila	Ceiceliah
Cecile	Ceil
Cécile	Ceila

Ceilagh	Celli
Ceileh	Cellie
Ceileigh	Celt
Ceilena	Celtic
Ceilí	Cendrillon
Ceilia	Cendrine
Ceilidh	Cenerentola
Ceindrech	Ceo
Ceinlys	Cera
Ceinwen	Ceradwyn
Ceira	Cerea
Ceiridwen	Ceredwyn
Ceirios	Ceri
Cela	Cerian
Cele	Cerice
Celeste	Cericia
Celia	Ceridwen
Celie	Ceridwyn
Celina	Cerie
Célina	Ceris
Celine	Cerisa
Céline	Cerise

Cerissa	Chana
Cerisse	Chandal
Cerria	Chandel
Cerridwen	Chandelier
Cerridwyn	Chandelle
Cerrina	Chandlar
Cerrita	Chandler
Cersei	Chandra
Ceryce	Chanel
Cerys	Chanele
Cesarine	Chanell
Cescelia	Chanelle
Cescelie	Chaney
Cescily	Channell
Cesia	Channelle
Cesilie	Chanta
Cesya	Chantaal
Cezanne	Chantae
Chablis	Chantael
Chainey	Chantai
Chambray	Chantal
Chamonix	Chantall

Chantalle	Chantil
Chantara	Chantila
Chantarai	Chantill
Chantasia	Chantille
Chantay	Chantilly
Chantaye	Chantle
Chante	Chanton
Chantea	Chantoya
Chanteau	Chantra
Chantee	Chantrel
Chanteese	Chantrell
Chantel	Chantrelle
Chantela	Chantress
Chantele	Chantri
Chantell	Chantrice
Chantella	Chantriel
Chantelle	Chantrill
Chanter	Chapin
Chantey	Charalin
Chantez	Charalyn
Chantiel	Charalynne
Chantielle	Chardonay

Chardonnay

Charee

Charelin

Charelyn

Charelynn

Charilyn

Charilynn

Charis

Charisse

Charity

Charlee

Charleigh

Charlene

Charlette

Charley

Charli

Charlie

Charlize

Charlot

Charlotte

Charmaine

Charnell

Chasity

Chaucer

Chaunta

Chauntay

Chaunte

Chauntel

Chauntell

Chauntelle

Chavonne

Chawntelle

Chaya

Chayney

Cheerish

Chelle

Chelsea

Chelsey

Chelsie

Chenelle

Chenille

Cher

Cheralin

Cheralyn

Chere

Cherece

Cheree

Chereen

Chereena

Chereese

Cherelle

Cherena

Cherene

Cheresa

Cherese

Cheresse

Cherey

Cheri

Cherice

Cherie

Cheriese

Cherilin

Cherilyn

Cherilynne

Cherina

Cherisa

Cherise

Cherish

Cherishe

Cherisse

Cherita

Cherralyn

Cherree

Cherrelle

Cherrey

Cherrice

Cherrie

Cherrilin

Cherrilyn

Cherrise

Cherrish

Cherry

Cherrylene

Cherrylin

Cherryline

Cherrylyn

Chery

Cheryce

Cherye	Chloé
Cheryl	Chonda
Cheryle	Chontel
Cherylie	Christa
Cherylin	Christel
Cheryllyn	Christelle
Cheryse	Christen
Cherysh	Christi
Cheryth	Christian
Chevelle	Christiana
Chevis	Christiane
Chevonne	Christie
Cheyanne	Christin
Cheyenne	Christina
Cheyrie	Christine
Chiara	Christy
Chiffon	Chrysanthe
Chimene	Chrystal
Chimere	Chyvonne
Chisholm	Ciaera
Chivon	Ciaira
Chloe	Cianna

Ciannait	Cinderella
Ciar	Cindy
Ciara	Cinniúint
Ciarah	Cissie
Ciarra	Citlali
Ciarrah	Citlalli
Cicelie	Citlaly
Cici	Citron
Cicilia	Claire
Cicilie	Clairette
Cicily	Cláirseoir
Cieara	Clara
Ciel	Claral
Cielo	Clare
Cienna	Clarette
Ciera	Clarissa
Cierra	Clarke
Cile	Claude
Cili	Claudelle
Cilka	Claudette
Cilla	Claudia
Cilly	Claudie

Claudine	Coleane
Clef	Coleene
Clemance	Colene
Clemence	Coleta
Clémence	Colette
Clementine	Coligny
Cleo	Coll
Clidhna	Colleen
Cliodhna	Collet
Cliona	Colleta
Clodagh	Collete
Clothilde	Collette
Clover	Collins
Cochran	Colombe
Coco	Columba
Codee	Colwyn
Codi	Comfort
Coeur	Comiskey
Coffey	Comyna
Coiréil	Conary
Colbie	Conleth
Colean	Connery

Connie	Cornelie
Constance	Corri
Cooper	Corrianna
Coquette	Corrigan
Cora	Cortenay
Coral	Corteney
Coralie	Cortne
Coraline	Cortnee
Corbeau	Cortneigh
Corcoran	Cortney
Cordelia	Cortnie
Cordney	Cortny
Cordni	Corwin
Corentine	Cory
Corey	Cosette
Cori	Coty
Coriann	Courteneigh
Corianne	Courteney
Corina	Courteny
Corinna	Courtlyn
Corinne	Courtnee
Corneille	Courtney

Courtnie	Curtis
Courtny	Cushla
Creideamh	Cyara
Creis	Cyarah
Creissant	Cyarra
Crescence	Cybele
Crescent	Cybille
Crescenta	Cynthia
Crescentia	Cyrielle
Cress	Cyrille
Cressant	D
Cressent	D'Or
Cressentia	Dacey
Cressentya	Daenerys
Cristal	Daffodil
Cristina	Dafne
Croía	Dahlia
Crwys	Dahra
Crystal	Dahrah
Crystin	Daicee
Cuileann	Daicy
Currier	Daija

Dailey	Danae
Daily	Dandelion
Dailyn	Danelle
Daimhin	Danelly
Daira	Danette
Daireann	Dangereuse
Daisey	Dani
Daisy	Dania
Dakota	Danica
Dalary	Danice
Daley	Daniela
Daleyza	Daniéle
Dalia	Daniella
Daliah	Danielle
Dalila	Danika
Dalilah	Danique
Dallas	Danna
Daly	Danon
Damari	Dany
Damaris	Daphne
Damica	Dara
Dana	Darah

Daralea	Darice
Daralee	Dariela
Daraleigh	Darilyn
Daraley	Darilyna
Daralyn	Darisa
Daray	Darissa
Darbie	Darka
Darby	Darla
Darcee	Darleen
Darceigh	Darlene
Darcelle	Darlyn
Darchelle	Darra
Darci	Darrell
Darcia	Darren
Darcie	Darsee
Darcy	Darseigh
Darda	Darsi
Dardah	Darsie
Dareau	Darya
Daria	Daryl
Dariana	Dasey
Dariann	Dasha

Davan	Deadra
Daveen	Deana
Daveney	Deanna
Davia	Dearbhail
Daviana	Dearbhla
Daviane	Debbie
Davianna	Debonaire
Davida	Debora
Davide	Deborah
Davidina	Debra
Davignon	Dede
Davina	Dedie
Davine	Dedra
Davinia	Dee
Davita	Deeana
Davynn	DeeDee
Dawn	Deedra
Dayana	Deedre
Dayanara	Deidra
Dayanna	Deidre
Dayna	Deidrea
Dayra	Deidrie

Deilf	Delene
Deirbhealla	DeLeon
Deirbhile	Delia
Deirdra	Délice
Deirdre	Delight
Deirdrea	Delilah
Deja	Della
Déja	Delma
DeLaina	Delmare
Delaine	Delphine
Delana	Delta
Delancey	Delwyn
Delancie	Delylah
Delancy	Delyth
Delaney	Demara
Delania	Demee
Delanie	Demi
Delaware	Demia
DeLayna	Demiana
Delayne	Demie
Deleine	Dena
Delena	Denali

Dency	Derby
Deneigh	Derdre
Denese	Deren
Deney	Derhyn
Deni	Deron
Denice	Derran
Deniece	Derrine
Denim	Derry
Denisa	Derrynne
Denise	Derval
Denissa	Dervla
Denisse	Deryn
Denize	Desarae
Dennette	Desi
Denni	Desideria
Dennise	Desirae
Dennison	Desire
Denver	Desiree
Denyce	Desirée
Denyse	Desiri
Denyw	Dessert
Deòiridh	Destanee

Destina	Devyn
Destine	Dewey
Destinee	Dewi
Destiney	Deyci
Destini	Diamant
Destinie	Diamond
Destiny	Diana
Destyni	Diane
Devan	Dianna
Devaney	Didiane
Devanie	Didina
Devany	Diedra
Devenny	Diedre
Deveraux	Diedrey
Devereaux	Diella
Devin	Dielle
Devina	Diem
Devinee	Dierdra
Devinne	Dierdre
Devon	Dil
Devony	Dileas
Devvin	Dillen

Dilly	Dolphin
Dillyn	Dominique
Dillys	Dominque
Dilwen	Domitilla
Dilwyn	Domitille
Dilys	Domonique
Dimanche	Donalda
Dina	Donaldette
Dinah	Donaldina
Dinnie	Donaline
Dionne	Donatienne
Dior	Donelda
Divine	Donella
Divinia	Donetta
Dixee	Donia
Dixie	Donita
Diya	Donna
Dóchas	Dora
Dodd	Dorann
Doireann	Doré
Dolie	Doreen
Dolores	Dorette

Dorielle	Durelle
Doris	Dusty
Doro	Dwana
Dorotea	Dwayna
Dorothée	Dwyn
Dorothy	Dwynwen
Dorsea	Dylan
Dory	Dylana
Douce	Dylane
Dream	Dylis
Drew	Dyllis
Dryw	Dylyd
Duana	Dymphna
Duayna	Dympna
Dubheasa	Ea
Dublin	Eabha
Duff	Éabha
Duffy	Eabhair
Dulce	Eachna
Dulcet	Eadaoin
Dulcette	Eadoin
Duna	Éala

Ealga	Eibhilin
Eamhair	Eibhleann
Eanid	Eibhlin
Eavan	Eiddwen
Ebony	Eila
Ebril	Eileen
Ebrill	Eilene
Ebrilla	Eilidh
Ebrillwen	Eilir
Ecgwynn	Eilis
Eden	Eilís
Edie	Eilish
Edith	Eilley
Ednah	Eilonwy
Edris	Eiluned
Edwige	Eimear
Eedris	Eimhear
Eevette	Eimy
Efa	Einin
Effie	Eira
Eglantine	Eire
Egypt	Eirian

Eirianwen	Eleri
Eirlys	Eleyn
Eirwen	Elfie
Eirwyn	Elia
Eiry	Elian
Eisley	Eliana
Eithne	Éliane
Eiza	Elianna
Ela	Elie
Elain	Eliette
Elaina	Elif
Elaine	Elin
Elara	Elina
Elayna	Elined
Eleanor	Elinor
Eleanora	Elinore
Eleanore	Elisa
Elen	Elisabeth
Elena	Elisaria
Eleni	Elise
Élénora	Elish
Eléonore	Elisha

Elissa	Élodie
Eliyanah	Eloisa
Eliza	Eloise
Elizabella	Elora
Elizabeth	Elowen
Elizah	Elsa
Elize	Elsbet
Ella	Elsbeth
Elle	Elsi
Ellen	Elsie
Ellery	Elspet
Ellia	Elspeth
Elliana	Elspie
Ellianna	Elsy
Ellie	Eluned
Elliot	Elva
Elliott	Elvéra
Ellis	Elvia
Ellison	Elvie
Elliw	Elvira
Elly	Elvire
Elodie	Elvy

Elyana	Emery
Elyse	Emi
Elysia	Emiko
Elyssa	Emilee
Ema	Emilia
Emani	Emiliana
Emarie	Emilie
Ember	Émilie
Emberly	Émilienne
Emele	Emily
Emelia	Emlyn
Emelie	Emm
Emeline	Emma
Emely	Emmalee
Emer	Emmaline
Emerald	Emmalyn
Emeraude	Emmalynn
Emerence	Emmanuelle
Emeri	Emmarie
Emerie	Emmarose
Emerson	Emme
Emersyn	Emmeline

Emmi	Ennis
Emmie	Ennish
Emmy	Ennya
Emogen	Enora
Emogene	Enright
Emory	Ensley
Emrie	Enya
Emry	Enyd
Ena	Enydd
Enah	Enye
Enda	Eos
Ened	Épiphanie
Enedd	Epona
Enedina	Eponine
Eneida	Eriana
Enfys	Erianna
Engracia	Erica
Enia	Ericka
Enid	Erika
Enidd	Erin
Enit	Erinna
Enna	Erinne

Eris	Esphyr
Erisha	Esprit
Erlina	Essyllt
Ermentrude	Esta
Ermine	Estee
Erminne	Estée
Errigal	Estefana
Erté	Estefania
Eryl	Estefany
Eryn	Estela
Erynn	Estelia
Erynna	Estelita
Eseld	Estella
Esma	Estelle
Esmae	Ester
Esme	Esther
Esmé	Estrella
Esmee	Esyllt
Esmeralda	Etain
Esmerie	Eternity
Esperance	Ethna
Esperanza	Ethnah

Ethnea	Évariste
Ethnee	Eve
Etienette	Evelin
Etoile	Evelina
Étoile	Evelyn
Eton	Evelyne
Etta	Evelynn
Eugenie	Ever
Eugénie	Everest
Eulalie	Everlee
Euna	Everleigh
Eunice	Everley
Euphème	Everly
Eva	Evette
Evaine	Evie
Evalina	Evlin
Evalyn	Evolet
Evalynn	Evonna
Evan	Evonne
Evangelina	Evony
Evangeline	Eyvetta
Evanna	Eyvette

Eyvonne	Faun
Ezra	Fauna
Fabienne	Faunia
Fabiola	Fawn
Fae	Fawna
Faedra	Fawne
Faela	Fawnia
Faerie	Fawnya
Faina	Fayanna
Fainche	Faye
Faith	Fayetta
Fallan	Faylinn
Fallen	Fedelma
Fallon	Feeona
Fallyn	Felicia
Fána	Felicienne
Fanchon	Félicité
Faraday	Felicity
Farah	Felipan
Farley	Fen
Farrah	Fenella
Fatima	Fennella

Feona	Fidelma
Ferelith	Fifi
Ferenc	Filia
Fern	Filippa
Fernanda	Finelia
Fernande	Finella
Fews	Finlay
Fey	Finley
Ffan	Finna
Ffion	Finnegan
Ffiona	Finnley
Fflur	Finola
Ffraid	Fion
Ffyona	Fiona
Fharly	Fional
Fhazaar	Fione
Fia	fionn
Fiachra	Fionna
Fiadh	Fionnah
Fíadh	Fionne
Fiana	Fionnoula
Fianna	Fionnuala

Fionnualagh	Floressa
Fionnula	Flori
Fionola	Flower
Fiorella	Flynn
Flana	Foighne
Flanagh	Foley
Flann	Fómhar
Flanna	Fonn
Flannerey	Fontanne
Flannery	Foraois
Flaviana	Forest
Flavie	France
Flaviere	Frances
Flavyere	Francesca
Fleur	Francessca
Fleurette	Francine
Fleurine	Francis
Flinn	Françoise
Flor	Franette
Flora	Frankie
Flore	Fraoch
Florence	Frazer

Frédérique

Fredy

Freya

Freyja

Frida

Frostine

Fruma

Fuinseog

Fynella

Fyona

Fyoni

Fyonie

Gabie

Gabrianna

Gabriela

Gabriella

Gabrielle

Gaby

Gael

Gaelle

Gaenna

Gaenor

Gaetane

Gai

Gaia

Gail

Gailyn

Gaiwan

Gala

Galaxy

Gale

Gali

Galilea

Galileah

Gaofar

Garan

Gardenia

Gareth

Garlande

Garldina

Garnet

Gavin

Gavyn

Gay

Gayana	Genevra
Gayna	Genevre
Gaynor	Génie
Gealach	Genifer
Geall	Geniffer
GeeGee	Genivee
Geimhreadh	Geniver
Gem	Genivieve
Gema	Genivra
Gemma	Genneigh
Genavee	Genney
Genavieve	Genni
Genesis	Gennie
Geneva	Gennifer
Geneve	Genniver
Genève	Gennivre
Geneveeve	Genny
Genever	Gennye
Genevia	Genovefa
Genevie	Genoveffa
Genevieve	Genovera
Geneviève	Genoveva

Geny	Gillian
Georgette	Gina
Georgia	Ginebra
Georgienne	Ginevra
Georgina	Ginevre
Geraldine	Ginger
Gerardine	Ginnie
Germaine	Gio
Gervaise	Giovanna
Gethwine	Girl's Name
Gezelle	Gisela
Ghislaine	Gisele
Gia	Giselle
Giada	Gislaine
Giana	Gisselle
Gianetta	Gitta
Gianna	Gitte
Gianni	Giulia
Giavanna	Giuliana
Gigi	Giulianna
Gilberte	Giulietta
Gilda	Gizelle

Glad

Gladdis

Gladdys

Gladi

Gladis

Gladys

Gladyss

Glaedwine

Glain

Gleana

Glema

Glen

Glenda

Gleneen

Glenene

Glenice

Glenine

Glenis

Glenn

Glenna

Glennda

Glenne

Glennene

Glennette

Glennice

Glennis

Glennys

Glenys

Glinda

Glinnis

Glinyce

Glinys

Glinyss

Gloria

Glory

Glyn

Glynae

Glynda

Glynice

Glynis

Glynn

Glynnis

Goldie

Goleu

Goleudydd

Gormlaith

Grace

Gracee

Gracelyn

Gracelynn

Gracey

Gracia

Gracie

Graciela

Graciella

Gracina

Grainne

Grainnia

Grania

Grásta

Grazielle

Grear

Grecia

Greer

Greta

Gretchen

Grettel

Grey

Grier

Griselda

Grisell

Gronia

Gry

Gryta

Guadalupe

Guendolen

Guendolin

Guendolinn

Guendolynn

Guenever

Guenevere

Gueniver

Guenivere

Guenna

Guennola

Guilette

Guillaumette

Guillaumine

Guin

Guinever

Guinevere

Guinna

Gurnoor

Gwawr

Gwen

Gwenaelle

Gwenda

Gwendal

Gwendaline

Gwendalyn

Gwendalynn

Gwenddydd

Gwendolen

Gwendolene

Gwendolin

Gwendoline

Gwendolyn

Gwendolynn

Gwendolynne

Gwendydd

Gweneth

Gwenetta

Gwenette

Gwenever

Gwenevere

Gwenhevare

Gwenhwyfar

Gwenifer

Gwenifrewi

Gwenisha

Gwenita

Gwenith

Gweniver

Gwenllian

Gwenn

Gwenna

Gwennan

Gwenndolen

Gwenness

Gwenneth

Gwennetta

Gwenni

Gwennie	Gwylan
Gwenno	Gwynda
Gwennol	Gwyndolyn
Gwennola	Gwynedd
Gwennor	Gwyneira
Gwennora	Gwyneth
Gwennore	Gwynevere
Gwenny	Gwynith
Gwenora	Gwynna
Gwenore	Gwynne
Gwenyth	Gwynneth
Gwerfyl	Gwynyth
Gwineth	Habika
Gwinna	Hadad
Gwinne	Hadara
Gwinneth	Hadassah
Gwinyth	Hadia
Gwir	Hadlee
Gwladus	Hadleigh
Gwladys	Hadley
Gwledyr	Haf
Gwyladyss	Hafwen

Hailee	Harlowe
Hailey	Harlyn
Hailie	Harmoni
Haisley	Harmony
Haleigh	Harper
Haley	Harriet
Halle	Harriette
Hallie	Hartley
Halo	Harvey
Halsey	Hattie
Hana	Havana
Haniya	Haven
Hanna	Hawa
Hannah	Haya
Happy	Hayden
Hardwinn	Haylee
Harlee	Hayley
Harleen	Haylie
Harleigh	Hazel
Harley	Heather
Harlie	Heaven
Harlow	Heavenly

Heeral	Hollie
Heidi	Hollis
Heidy	Holly
Helaine	Honesty
Heledd	Honey
Helen	Honor
Helena	Honore
Helene	Honoré
Hellen	Hood
Hellena	Hope
Heloise	Hosanna
Héloïse	Hudson
Henley	Huguette
Hennessy	Hunter
Henrietta	Hunydd
Henriette	Husna
Heulwen	Hyacinth
Hilaire	Hyacinthe
Hilary	Ibb
Hillary	Ibbie
Hlynn	Ibukun
Holland	Ida

Ide

Idelisa

Idella

Idelle

Idris

Ieasha

Ieni

Igraine

Ihisha

Ila

Ilana

Ilanis

Ilanys

Ilar

Ileana

Ilene

Iliana

Illiana

Illuminée

Ilona

Iman

Imani

Immy

Imogen

Imogene

Imogenia

Imogine

Imojean

Imojeen

Ina

Inaaya

Inara

Inaya

Inayah

Indeg

India

Indiana

Indie

Indigo

Indre

Ine

Ines

Inez

Ingenue

Ingrid	Irma
Innis	Isa
Innogen	Isabeau
Ioanna	Isabel
Iolanthe	Isabela
Iona	Isabell
Ione	Isabella
Ioni	Isabelle
Ionia	Isabelline
Iorwen	Isadora
Iphigenie	Isaline
Ira	Iseabail
Irecia	Isela
Ireland	Isha
Irelynn	Ishika
Irene	Isis
Iridia	Isla
Irie	Islay
Iris	Isleen
Irisa	Ismay
Irisha	Isobel
Irlanda	Isolde

Issa	Izabella
Ita	Izabelle
Italia	Izel
Italy	Izett
Itzamara	Izod
Itzayana	Jaba
Itzel	Jacalin
Itzia	Jacalyn
Iva	Jacalynn
Ivana	Jacenta
Ivanka	Jacey
Ivanna	Jacinta
Ivett	Jacinthe
Ivetta	Jackalin
Ivette	Jackalinne
Ivonna	Jackeline
Ivonne	Jackelyn
Ivory	Jacketta
Ivy	Jackette
Iyla	Jackie
Izabel	Jacklin
Izabela	Jacklyn

Jacklynn	Jacquelynne
Jacklynne	Jacquenetta
Jackqueline	Jacquenette
Jaclin	Jacquetta
Jaclyn	Jacquette
Jacolyn	Jacqui
Jacqi	Jacquie
Jacqlyn	Jacquine
Jacqualine	Jacquotte
Jacqualyn	Jaculine
Jacquard	Jada
Jacquel	Jade
Jacquelean	Jaden
Jacqueleen	Jadyn
Jacquelin	Jael
Jacquelina	Jaelyn
Jacqueline	Jaelynn
Jacquella	Jaida
Jacquelle	Jaiden
Jacquelyn	Jailyne
Jacquelyne	Jaime
Jacquelynn	Jakleen

Jaklyn	Janevra
Jaliyah	Janez
James	Janice
Jameson	Janie
Jami	Janifer
Jamie	Janine
Jamila	Janit
Jamileth	Janiya
Jana	Janiyah
Janae	Janna
Jane	Jannet
Janella	Janneth
Janelle	Jannette
Janelly	Janney
Janessa	Janos
Janet	Janot
Janeta	Janvier
Janeth	Jaquelin
Janett	Jaqueline
Janetta	Jaquelyn
Janette	Jaquelynn
Janeva	Jaquith

Jaretzy	Jaylyn
Jarrell	Jaylynn
Jasleen	Jayme
Jaslene	Jayne
Jaslyn	Jazelle
Jasmin	Jazleen
Jasmine	Jazlene
Jaycee	Jazlyn
Jaycie	Jazlynn
Jayda	Jazmin
Jayde	Jazmine
Jayden	Jazmyn
Jayla	Jazzlyn
Jaylah	Jean
Jaylani	Jeane
Jaylee	Jeanetta
Jayleen	Jeanette
Jaylen	Jeanine
Jaylene	Jeanne
Jaylie	Jeannette
Jaylin	Jeannie
Jayline	Jehanne

Jelena	Jenna
Jemma	Jennalee
Jen	Jennalyn
Jena	Jennavieve
Jenalee	Jenne
Jenalyn	Jennea
Jenavieve	Jennee
Jenefer	Jennefer
Jenelle	Jenneigh
Jenesis	Jennet
Jeneth	Jennette
Jenetta	Jenneva
Jenette	Jenney
Jeneva	Jenni
Jenevieve	Jennica
Jeni	Jennie
Jenibelle	Jennifar
Jenifer	Jennifer
Jeniffer	Jenniffer
Jenita	Jennika
Jenlyns	Jennipher
Jenn	Jenniver

Jenny	Jewelyn
Jennyfer	Jhene
Jenovefa	Jia
Jenyfer	Jianna
Jermaine	Jill
Jesiah	Jillian
Jeslyn	Jimena
Jessa	Jineeva
Jessamine	Jineva
Jessi	Jinnet
Jessica	Jinnett
Jessie	Jiselle
Jesslyn	Jiya
Jesstina	Jo-Dell
Jestina	Joan
Jestine	Joana
Jeune	Joann
Jewel	Joanna
Jewelene	Joanne
Jewelisa	Jocelin
Jewella	Jocelyn
Jewelle	Jocelyne

Jocelynn

Jodell

Jodelle

Jodi

Jodie

Jody

Joela

Joelin

Joella

Joelle

Joellen

Joelliane

Joellin

Joelly

Joellyn

Joely

Joelynn

Joetta

Joey

Johana

Johanna

Johnetta

Johnette

Joie

Jolee

Joleigh

Jolene

Joley

Jolie

Joliet

Jolietta

Joliette

Joly

Jonette

Joneva

Jonevah

Joni

Jonilde

Jonquille

Jooley

Joolie

Jordan

Jordane

Jordyn

Jordynn	Jowella
Josée	Jowelle
Josefina	Joy
Joselin	Joyce
Joselyn	Juanita
Josephe	Jubilee
Josephina	Jude
Josephine	Judith
Josette	Juditha
Josiane	Judithe
Josie	Judy
Joslyn	Juelline
Josselyn	Juillet
Josslyn	Juin
Jourdain	Jules
Jourdaine	Juli
Journee	Julia
Journey	Juliana
Journi	Julianna
Jovianne	Julianne
Jovie	Julie
Jovienne	Julienne

Juliet	Kaare
Julieta	Kace
Julieth	Kacee
Julietta	Kacey
Juliette	Kaci
Julissa	Kacie
Jullee	Kacye
Jullie	Kacyee
Jully	Kaddy
Jumeaux	Kadence
Jumelle	Kadi
Juna	Kady
June	Kaela
Juneau	Kaelah
Juniper	Kaelani
Juno	Kaelyn
Jurnee	Kaelynn
Justice	Kaetlyn
Justine	Kahla
K.C.	Kai
Kaala	Kaia
Kaara	Kaidence

Kaila	Kalani
Kailagh	Kalea
Kailah	Kaleah
Kailani	Kaleigh
Kailee	Kalena
Kaileigh	Kaley
Kailey	Kali
Kailie	Kalia
Kaily	Kaliah
Kailyn	Kalila
Kaira	Kalina
Kairi	Kaliyah
Kaisley	Kallan
Kaissie	Kalley
Kait	Kallie
Kaitlin	Kally
Kaitlinn	Kamari
Kaitlyn	Kameren
Kaitlynn	Kamerin
Kaiya	Kameron
Kalae	Kameryn
Kalah	Kamila

Kamilah

Kamilla

Kamille

Kamiyah

Kammeron

Kamren

Kamrin

Kamryn

Kamrynn

Kamrynne

Kamyron

Kandra

Kara

Karely

Karen

Kari

Karin

Karina

Karis

Karisma

Karissa

Karla

Karlee

Karley

Karli

Karlie

Karly

Karma

Karolina

Karoline

Karsyn

Karter

Karys

Kasci

Kasee

Kasey

Kasidy

Kassadey

Kassadi

Kassandra

Kassidee

Kassidi

Kassidie

Kassidy

Kassodey	Kathleena
Kasy	Kathlena
Kat	Kathlene
Kataleya	Kathleyn
Katalina	Kathlin
Katarina	Kathline
Kate	Kathlyn
Katell	Kathlynn
Katelyn	Kathryn
Katelynn	Kathy
Katerina	Kathyline
Katha	Kathylyne
Kathaleen	Katia
Kathaleya	Katie
Kathaleyna	Katina
Kathaline	Katleen
Kathan	Katline
Katharine	Katlyn
Kathelina	Katlyne
Katheline	Katrina
Katherine	Katriona
Kathleen	Katy

Katya	Kayli
Kavya	Kaylie
Kay	Kaylin
Kaya	Kaylla
Kayce	Kaylyn
Kaycee	Kaylynn
Kaycey	Kayse
Kayci	Kaysee
Kaycie	Kaysey
Kayden	Kaysi
Kaydence	Kaysie
Kayla	Kaysy
Kaylah	Kaysyee
Kaylani	KC
Kayle	Keagan
Kaylee	Keaira
Kayleen	Keana
Kayleigh	Keara
Kaylen	Keavy
Kaylene	Keeana
Kayley	Keearra
Kaylha	Keegan

Keela	Kelianne
Keelan	Kella
Keeley	Kellee
Keelin	Kelleen
Keelty	Kelleigh
Keely	Kellen
Keena	Kelley
Keeran	Kelli
Keeva	Kellie
Keevah	Kellina
Kegan	Kelly
Kehlani	Kellyann
Keila	Kellyanne
Keilani	Kellye
Keily	Kellyn
Keir	Kelsea
Keira	Kelsey
Keiry	Kelsie
Keisha	Keltie
Keitha	Kena
Kekilia	Kenadie
Kel	Kenda

Kendall

Kendra

Kendrah

Kendrea

Kendri

Kendria

Kendrie

Kendrya

Keni

Kenia

Kenina

Kenley

Kenna

Kennah

Kenndra

Kenndrea

Kennedi

Kennedy

Kensington

Kensley

Kenya

Kenza

Kenzie

Kenzy

Keonna

Kera

Keree

Keri

Keriana

Keriann

Kerianna

Kerianne

Kerilyn

Kerin

Kerr

Kerra

Kerri

Kerria

Kerrianne

Kerridana

Kerrin

Kerry

Kerryn

Keryn

Keturah	Kiera
Keva	Kieran
Kevia	Kierra
Kevina	Kiersten
Kevine	Kieve
Kevinne	Kikelia
Kevynn	Kiki
Kevynne	Kikylia
Keyla	Kilee
Keyna	Kiley
Keziah	Killian
Khadija	Kim
Khalani	Kimber
Khaleesi	Kimberlee
Khalia	Kimberley
Khari	Kimberly
Khloe	Kimora
Kiah	Kincaid
Kiana	Kingsley
Kiandra	Kinley
Kianna	Kinna
Kiara	Kinsey

Kinslee

Kinsley

Kinzie

Kinzley

Kira

Kirra

Kirstee

Kirsten

Kirsti

Kirstie

Kirsty

Kitty

Kiva

Klarissa

Koda

Kodee

Kody

Kora

Kordney

Kori

Korie

Korra

Korri

Kortney

Kortni

Kourtenay

Kourtnee

Kourtneigh

Kourtney

Kourtnie

Krisha

Krista

Kristal

Kristen

Kristi

Kristie

Kristin

Kristina

Kristine

Kristy

Krystal

Krystle

Kya

Kyall

Kyara	Lacy
Kyel	Lacyann
Kyla	Lady
Kylah	Lafayette
Kyle	Laicee
Kylee	Laicey
Kyleigh	Laila
Kylie	Lailah
Kyndra	Lailani
Kyndria	Laili
Kynlee	Lainey
Kyra	Laisey
Kyrie	Lakeisha
Lace	Lakendra
Lacee	Lakisha
Lacene	Lana
Lacey	Landry
Lachann	Lanette
Lachlan	Laney
Laci	Lani
Laciann	Laniyah
Lacklan	Laoghaire

Laoise	Latisha
Laomedon	Latonya
Lara	Latoya
Laraine	Laughlin
Laramie	Laura
Lareina	Laure
Larhonda	Laurel
Larissa	Lauren
Laronda	Laurentina
Larue	Laurentyna
Lasair	Laurentyne
Lasee	Laurette
Lasey	Laurie
Lasi	Laurraine
Lasie	Lauryn
Lassee	Lavaughan
Lassey	Lave
Lassi	Lavender
Lassie	Laverne
Lassy	Laya
Lasy	Layah
Latasha	Layan

Laycie	Legacy
Layla	Leia
Laylah	Leiana
Laylani	Leifur
Layne	Leigh
Lea	Leighton
Léa	Leila
Leah	Leilah
Leal	Leilani
Leala	Leilanie
Lealia	Leilany
Lealie	Leithe
Leana	Lela
Leann	Lena
Leanna	Lenette
Leanne	Lennon
LeBlanc	Lennox
Lee	Lenore
Leela	Leona
Leelee	Léonette
Leen	Leonie
Leena	Léonie

Léonne	Leylah
Leontina	Leylani
Leontine	Lezlee
Leontyne	Lezley
Leopoldine	Lezlie
Leraine	Lia
Lerayne	Líadáin
Leslee	Liadan
Lesleigh	Liah
Lesley	Liahna
Lesli	Lian
Leslie	Liana
Lesly	Liandan
Lethe	Liane
Leticia	Liann
Leven	Lianna
Leverett	Lianne
Levron	Libby
Lexa	Liberty
Lexi	Lidia
Lexie	Lieselotte
Leyla	Lieux

Lila	Lillyana
Lilac	Lillyanna
Lilah	Lilou
Lilas	Lily
Lileas	Lilyana
Lili	Lilyanna
Lilia	Lina
Lilian	Lincoln
Liliana	Linda
Liliane	Lindsay
Lilianna	Lindsey
Lilias	Linet
Lilit	Linett
Lilith	Linetta
Lillas	Linette
Lillian	Linnea
Lilliana	Linnet
Lillianna	Linnette
Lillias	Linnit
Lillie	Linniue
Lillith	Lionel
Lilly	Liora

Lisa	Lochlyn
Lisette	Lock
Lisle	Lockie
Litzy	Logan
Liv	Logann
Livia	Loie
Liya	Loire
Liyana	Lois
Liz	Lola
Liza	London
Lizbeth	Londyn
Lizeth	Lonette
Lizette	Lora
Lleucu	Lorain
Llewella	Loraina
Lleyke	Loraine
Llinos	Lorayne
Lluvia	Lorelai
Llyn	Lorelei
Llywelya	Loren
Llywelydd	Lorena
Lochellen	Loreto

Loretta

Lori

Lorna

Lorraina

Lorraine

Lorrayne

Lorrna

Lottie

Lotus

Lou

Loucille

Louisa

Louise

Louisiana

Louisiane

Louisianna

Lourdecita

Lourdes

Lourdetta

Lourdette

Love

Lovely

Lowri

Lowry

Loyalty

Luca

Lucero

Lucette

Lucia

Luciana

Luciann

Lucianna

Lucida

Lucie

Luciela

Lucienne

Lucila

Lucille

Lucinda

Lucinde

Lucinenne

Lucrece

Lucrèce

Lucy

Lucyle	Lyla
Luella	Lylah
Lúil	Lyle
Luisa	Lyndsey
Lula	Lynelle
Lulu	Lynessa
Lumière	Lyneth
Luna	Lynett
Lúnasa	Lynetta
Lune	Lynette
Luned	Lynlea
Lunet	Lynn
Lunette	Lynnelle
Lupita	Lynnet
Lurdes	Lynnette
Luseele	Lyonell
Lusile	Lyons
Lux	Lyra
Luz	Lyric
Lyanna	Lyrica
Lydia	Lyricia
Lydie	Lys

Maaria	Madadh
Mab	Madalyn
Mabel	Madalynn
Mabli	Maddalena
Mabyn	Madden
Macall	Maddie
Macaulay	Maddison
Maccaulay	Madelaine
Macee	Madeleine
Macerio	Madeline
Macey	Madella
Macha	Madelle
Maci	Madelyn
Macie	Madelyne
Mackendra	Madelynn
Mackensi	Madigan
Mackenzey	Madilyn
Mackenzie	Madilynn
Mackie	Madison
Maclean	Madisyn
Macrae	Mado
Macy	Madrona

Madrun	Magdalena
Madyson	Magdalene
Mae	Maggie
Maebh	Magnolia
Maegan	Magritte
Maegen	Maha
Maela	Mahogany
Maelie	Mahoney
Maelle	Mai
Maelys	Maia
Maerwynn	Maicey
Maeva	Maicy
Maeve	Maigen
Maevi	Maighdlin
Magali	Maika
Magalie	Mailen
Magaly	Maili
Magan	Maille
Magdala	Mailys
Magdalaine	Maine
Magdaleine	Mair
Magdalen	Maira

Maire	Malayah
Mairead	Malaysia
Mairi	Malcolmina
Mairim	Maleah
Mairin	Malena
Mairwen	Mali
Maisie	Malia
Maite	Maliah
Maiti	Malina
Maiya	Malise
Majella	Maliya
Majesty	Maliyah
Makara	Mallaidh
Makayla	Mallary
Makena	Mallerey
Makenna	Malloree
Makensie	Malloreigh
Makenzi	Mallorey
Makenzie	Mallori
Malak	Mallory
Malani	Malorey
Malaya	Malori

Malorie	Marchery
Malvina	Marchesa
Mandere	Marchessa
Mandolin	Marcia
Mandy	Marcy
Maneh	Mardi
Manet	Mare
Manette	Marely
Mannat	Maren
Manon	Margaret
Maolisa	Margarita
Maple	Margaux
Mara	Margeaux
Maranda	Marged
Marared	Margeree
Marbella	Margerey
Marcela	Margery
Marcelia	Margherite
Marceline	Margi
Marcella	Margo
Marcelle	Margot
Marcheline	Marguerite

Margurite	Marien
Mari	Mariet
Maria	Marietta
Mariah	Mariette
Mariam	Marigold
Marian	Marilee
Mariana	Marilena
Marianda	Marilene
Mariane	Marilisa
Mariann	Marilou
Marianna	Marilu
Marianne	Marilyn
Maribel	Marina
Maribelle	Marine
Maribeth	Marion
Maricela	Marisa
Maridel	Marisol
Marie	Marissa
Mariel	Marita
Mariela	Maritza
Mariella	Mariyah
Marielle	Marjerie

Marjie	Marquisa
Marjo	Marquisha
Marjolaine	Marseilles
Marjolie	Marsha
Marjori	Martella
Marjorie	Martha
Marjy	Marthe
Markaisa	Martine
Markessa	Martinique
Marla	Marvel
Marlee	Marvene
Marleigh	Marwa
Marlene	Mary
Marlette	Maryam
Marley	Maryan
Marlie	Maryann
Marlow	Maryanna
Marlowe	Marycruz
Marnie	Maryetta
Marquesa	Maryjane
Marquessa	Maryon
Marquette	Maryonn

Mathilde	May
Matilda	Maya
Matilde	Mayah
Mattie	Mayeli
Maud	Maygan
Maude	Mayleen
Maura	Maylin
Maureen	Mayra
Maurelle	Mayte
Mauresa	Mazarine
Maurianne	Mazie
Maurice	Mazikeen
Maurisa	Mazine
Maurissa	Mazzy
Mauve	McCall
Mave	McClure
Maven	McCormick
Mavis	McCoy
Mavye	McCullough
Max	McDaniel
Maxime	McDonald
Maxine	McDowell

McGee	Meggie
McGuire	Meggy
Mckayla	Meghan
McKee	Meghann
Mckenna	Meghanne
Mckenzie	Mehar
Mckinley	Mei
McKinney	Meighan
Meabh	Meilani
Meadow	Meinir
Meagan	Meinwen
Meaghan	Meiriona
Mealla	Meirna
Meara	Meitheamh
Meave	Mélaine
Medi	Melangell
Meeghan	Melani
Meera	Melania
Megan	Melanie
Megen	Mélanie
Meggan	Melaniu
Meggi	Melannie

Melany	Mercy
Meleri	Meredith
Melia	Meredithe
Melina	Mererid
Melinda	Merial
Melisa	Merida
Melisande	Meriel
Mélisande	Merielle
Melisandre	Meriol
Melissa	Merl
Melissande	Merla
Mellicent	Merle
Mellisent	Merlin
Melodie	Merlina
Melody	Merline
Melusine	Merlyn
Melva	Merna
Melvina	Merola
Menna	Merouda
Meradith	Merridie
Mercedes	Merthyr
Mercer	Meryl

Metztli

Mhairi

Mia

Miabella

Miach

Miah

Micaela

Micah

Michael

Michaela

Michal

Michele

Michéle

Michèle

Micheline

Michelle

Michon

Michonne

Miette

Mignon

Mignonette

Mignonne

Mika

Mikaela

Mikayla

Mil

Mila

Milagro

Milagros

Milah

Milan

Milana

Milani

Milania

Mileena

Milena

Miley

Miliana

Milicent

Milisent

Milla

Millicent

Millie

Milly

Milzie	Mireille
Mimi	Mireio
Mina	Mirell
Mindy	Mirette
Minerva	Mireya
Minerve	Miriam
Minette	Mirielle
Mingnon	Mirna
Miniona	Mirren
Minjonet	Misha
Minuet	Mistique
Minuit	Misty
Minyonette	Miureall
Minyonne	Miya
Mira	Miyah
Mirabella	Moana
Mirabelle	Moina
Miracle	Moira
Mirage	Moire
Mirain	Mollee
Miranda	Molley
Mireilla	Molli

Mollie	Moreen
Molly	Morella
Mona	Morene
Monah	Morey
Monahan	Morfudd
Monalisa	Morgain
Monalissa	Morgaine
Monet	Morgan
Monica	Morgana
Monike	Morgance
Moniqua	Morgane
Monique	Morganica
Monna	Morgann
Monroe	Morganne
Monserrat	Morgayne
Monserrath	Morgen
Montserrat	Morgian
Moon	Morgin
Mora	Morgon
Morag	Moria
Morah	Moriah
Moran	Morine

Morna	Muirne
Morrigan	Muriel
Morven	Muriella
Morvyth	Murle
Morwen	Murna
Morwena	Murphey
Morwenna	Murphy
Morwina	Murron
Morwinna	Musetta
Morwyn	Musette
Morwynna	Mya
Mostyn	Myah
Moya	Myfanwy
Moyer	Myla
Moyna	Mylah
Muguet	Mylene
Muire	Myra
Muireall	Myrelle
Muireann	Myrl
Muirgan	Myrle
Muirgheal	Myrleen
Muirna	Myrlene

Myrline

Myrna

Myrtle

Mystica

Mystique

Mystral

Naava

Nadeen

Nadége

Nadena

Nadene

Nadia

Nadina

Nadine

Nadyna

Nadyne

Naeva

Naeveh

Nage

Nahla

Nahomi

Nahomy

Naia

Naila

Nailah

Naima

Naimh

Nairne

Nala

Nalani

Naliyah

Nancy

Nanée

Nanette

Nanine

Nannette

Nanon

Nanou

Naomh

Naomi

Naomy

Nara

Narcisse

Narguize

Narqis	Nealla
Natalee	Neamh
Natalène	Neelle
Natalia	Neely
Natalie	Neema
Nataly	Nefertari
Natalya	Nefyn
Natasha	Neige
Nathalia	Neilina
Nathalie	Neilla
Nathaly	Neiv
Nathara	Neive
Natividad	Nelina
Naveah	Nellie
Navy	Nelly
Navya	Neris
Naya	Neriss
Naydeen	Nerys
Nayeli	Neryss
Nayla	Ness
Nazayia	Nessa
Neala	Nest

Nesta	Nichelle
Nevaeh	Nichole
Nevan	Nicholina
Neve	Nico
Neveah	Nicole
Nevee	Nicoletta
Nevia	Nicolette
Neviah	Nicollette
Nevin	Nieve
Nevina	Nika
Neya	Nikita
Neyah	Nikki
Neyva	Nila
Neyve	Nimah
Nia	Nina
Niah	Ninette
Niajia	Ninian
Niall	Ninon
Niama	Nirvana
Niamah	Niya
Niamh	Niyah
Nichele	Noa

Noah	Nolana
Noe	Noland
Noel	Nolanda
Noela	Nolene
Noelani	Nollaig
Noele	Nolwenn
Noeleen	Nolynn
Noelene	Non
Noelia	Noor
Noeline	Noora
Noeliz	Nora
Noell	Norah
Noella	Noreen
Noelle	Noreena
Noelleen	Norene
Noely	Norinne
Noelynn	Norma
Noemi	Normandy
Noémie	Norris
Nohemi	Nour
Nóinín	Nouvel
Nola	Nova

Novah	Oceane
Novalee	Océane
Noweleen	Octava
Noyer	Octavia
Nuala	Octavie
Nya	Oda
Nyah	Odalis
Nyam	Odeletta
Nyama	Odessa
Nyamah	Odetta
Nyfain	Odette
Nyla	Odile
Nylah	Odilia
Nynette	Ofelia
Nyomi	Ofilia
Nyra	Oleesa
Oaklee	Oleisa
Oakleigh	Olga
Oakley	Olisa
Oaklyn	Olive
Oaklynn	Olivette
Ocean	Olivia

Oliviane	Oralia
Olwen	Oralie
Olwenn	Oran
Olwin	Orane
Olwyn	Orania
Olwyne	Oreli
Olwynne	Orelie
Olympe	Oriana
Olympia	Oriane
Olympiad	Orianne
Olympienne	Oriel
Ómra	Orielda
Ondelette	Orinthia
Ondine	Orla
Onyx	Orlagh
Oona	Orlah
Oonagh	Orlaith
Opal	Orleane
Opaque	Orleans
Ophelia	Orlee
Ophelie	Orlena
Ophélie	Orlene

Orly	Pandora
Ormanda	Pansy
Orra	Paola
Orrla	Papillon
Osla	Paris
Ottalia	Parker
Ottilie	Parlan
Ottolie	Parry
Ottoline	Pascale
Ouida	Pascalie
Owena	Pascaline
Ownah	Pascasia
Page	Pasquette
Paige	Patience
Paislee	Patrice
Paisleigh	Patricia
Paisley	Paula
Paityn	Paule
Palmer	Paulette
Paloma	Paulille
Pamela	Paulina
Paméla	Pauline

Pavanne	Percy
Payton	Peren
Peach	Perette
Pearl	Peridot
Péarla	Perla
Peg	Perle
Pegeen	Perlette
Peggie	Perline
Peggy	Pernella
Peigi	Péronelle
Peita	Perpétue
Peitil	Perrette
Pembroke	Perrey
Pendant	Perrine
Penelope	Persephone
Pennelope	Perweur
Penny	Petal
Penrose	Petit
Pensée	Petra
Peony	Petronille
Pépélope	Pétronille
Pepper	Petunia

Peyton	Polina
Phaedra	Pollee
Phalen	Polley
Phiala	Polli
Philippine	Pomeline
Philis	Pomme
Phillis	Poppy
Philomène	Porcie
Phoebe	Porter
Phoenix	Posie
Pia	Prairie
Piaf	Precious
Pierette	Preslee
Pierina	Presley
Pierra	Prew
Pierrette	Prewdence
Pilar	Pricilla
Piobar	Prim
Piper	Primevère
Pixie	Primrose
Placidie	Princess
Pleasance	Prisca

Priscila	Quincie
Priscilla	Quincy
Priscille	Quinlan
Prisha	Quinn
Priya	Quinnley
Promise	Quintessa
Provence	Rachael
Prudentiane	Rachel
Prudenzia	Rachelle
Prue	Racquel
Prune	Radha
Prunelle	Rae
Pugh	Raegan
Purnima	Raelene
Queen	Raelyn
Queena	Raelynn
Queenie	Raewyn
Quella	Rafaella
Questa	Rafaila
Quillan	Raffelle
Quin	Rafferty
Quinci	Ragan

Raimonda	Reagan
Rain	Réalta
Raina	Réaltra
Raine	Reanan
Ramona	Reanna
Ramonde	Reannah
Randi	Reanne
Rania	Reannon
Ranking	Réba
Raoule	Rebeca
Raphaëlle	Rebecca
Rapheala	Rébecca
Raquel	Rebekah
Raven	Reeanne
Raya	Reenie
Rayleen	Reese
Raylene	Reeva
Raylynn	Regan
Raymonde	Reghan
Raymondine	Regia
Rayna	Regina
Rayne	Régine

Reign	Rey
Reilly	Reya
Reina	Reyna
Reine	Rhea
Reinette	Rheana
Remi	Rheanna
Remington	Rheanne
Remy	Rhedyn
Renae	Rhemy
Renata	Rhett
Renate	Rhiain
Renaud	Rhian
Renay	Rhiana
Rene	Rhiane
Renee	Rhiann
Renée	Rhianna
Reneisha	Rhiannan
Renell	Rhiannon
Renesmee	Rhianon
Renny	Rhianu
Revanche	Rhianwen
Reverie	Rhianydd

Rhona	Riannon
Rhonda	Rianon
Rhondelle	Riayn
Rhondene	Rice
Rhondiesha	Richarde
Rhonette	Richelle
Rhonnda	Richilde
Rhonwen	Ridley
Rhoslyn	Riece
Rhoswen	Rigny
Rhosyn	Rihanna
Rhyan	Rikki
Rhylee	Rilee
Rhylen	Rileigh
Rhys	Riley
Ria	Rilynn
Rian	Rina
Riana	Rio
Riane	Ríoga
Riann	Riona
Rianna	Rionach
Rianne	Rionna

Rionnagh	Roisin
Rionnah	Róisín
Ripley	Rolande
Rita	Romaine
Rivage	Romanade
River	Romane
Rivka	Romanette
Riya	Romany
Robena	Romayne
Roberta	Romeine
Roberte	Romene
Robertina	Romi
Robin	Romilly
Robina	Romina
Robine	Romy
Robyn	Ronaldette
Roch	Ronaldine
Rochelle	Ronat
Rocio	Ronda
Roesia	Rondel
Rogue	Rondelle
Róinseach	Rondi

Ronee

Ronnda

Rori

Rory

Rós

Rosa

Rosabella

Rosalee

Rosaleen

Rosaley

Rosalia

Rosalie

Rosalina

Rosalind

Rosalinda

Rosalyn

Rosalyne

Rosalynn

Rosario

Rose

Roselle

Roselyn

Roselynn

Rosemarie

Rosemary

Rosemonda

Rosemonde

Rosette

Rosie

Rosine

Roslyn

Rosy

Rouge

Rousseau

Roux

Rowan

Rowe

Rowen

Rowena

Rowenna

Rowyn

Roxana

Roxanna

Roxanne

Roxy	Ruthven
Roya	Ryan
Royal	Ryana
Royalene	Ryane
Royalina	Ryann
Royalla	Ryanna
Royalle	Ryanne
Royalty	Ryder
Royalyn	Ryenne
Royalynne	Ryette
Royce	Rylan
Rozelie	Rylee
Rozelle	Ryleigh
Rozellia	Rylie
Rozely	Rylin
Rrenae	Rylina
Ruairí	Rynn
Rubi	Saanvi
Ruby	Saara
Ruhi	Sabella
Rumi	Sabia
Ruth	Sabienne

Sabina	Saisha
Sabine	Saison
Sable	Sakura
Sabrena	Salamanca
Sabrina	Salem
Sacha	Sally
Sacilia	Salma
Sadb	Salome
Sade	Salomé
Sadhbh	Sam
Sadie	Sama
Safa	Samaira
Saffron	Samantha
Sage	Samanthée
Sahana	Samanvi
Sahara	Samara
Sahasra	Samaya
Sai	Samhradh
Saige	Samira
Saileach	Samiyah
Sailor	Sana
Saira	Sanan

Sanaya	Sarotte
Sandra	Sash
Sandrine	Sasha
Sandy	Sasilia
Sanica	Sasilie
Saniyah	Satin
Santana	Satine
Sanvi	Saundra
Saoirse	Savanna
Saorsie	Savannah
Sapphire	Savina
Sara	Sawyer
Sarah	Saylor
Sarahi	Sayuri
Sarai	Scarlet
Saraid	Scarlett
Saray	Scarletta
Sarese	Scarlette
Sarette	Scherie
Sariah	Scota
Sarina	Scout
Sariyah	Scoutt

Seamair

Sean

Seana

Seanna

Seath

Sébastienne

Secelia

Sedona

Seelia

Seelie

Seerat

Sehaj

Seila

Selah

Selena

Selene

Selia

Selina

Selma

Sena

Senga

Senna

Seonald

Sequin

Sequoia

Serafina

Seraphina

Seraphine

Séraphine

Seren

Serena

Serene

Serenity

Serina

Sesilia

Sessaley

Sesseelya

Sessile

Sessilly

Sessily

Sessy

Seva

Sevastiane

Severin

Severine

Sevyn

Sh'vonne

Shadow

Shaela

Shaelyn

Shaila

Shaina

Shana

Shanaya

Shanda

Shandelle

Shane

Shanel

Shanell

Shania

Shanna

Shannan

Shannel

Shannelle

Shannon

Shantahl

Shantal

Shantalle

Shantel

Shantell

Shantella

Shantelle

Shanton

Sharalin

Sharalyn

Sharay

Shareese

Sharelyn

Sharelynne

Shari

Sharice

Sharilynn

Sharon

Shary

Sharyse

Shauna

Shaunda

Shaunta

Shauntell

Shavaun

Shawn

Shawna

Shawnda

Shawnta

Shawntile

Shawntille

Shay

Shayla

Shaylagh

Shaylah

Shaylee

Shaylla

Shayna

Shea

Sheehan

Sheela

Sheelagh

Sheelah

Sheena

Sheenagh

Sheenah

Sheila

Sheilagh

Sheilah

Sheileen

Sheilia

Sheilya

Sheirys

Shela

Shelagh

Shelah

Shelby

Shelia

Shella

Shelley

Shelly

Shena

Shenelle

Sher

Sheralin

Sheralynne

Sherece

Sheree

Shereece

Shereen

Shereena

Sherees

Shereese

Shereeza

Sherelle

Sheresa

Sherese

Sherey

Sherez

Sheri

Sheria

Sherice

Sheridan

Sheridon

Sheriesa

Sherilin

Sherise

Sherissa

Sherlyn

Sherralin

Sherrelle

Sherri

Sherrica

Sherrilyn

Sherry

Sherrylene

Sherryline

Sherrylyn

Sherryse

Shervan

Shery

Sheryl

Sherylin

Sherylyn

Shevon

Shevonne

Sheyla

Shiela

Shila

Shilah

Shilea

Shilla

Shiloh

Shinead

Shiona

Shionagh

Shira

Shirece

Shiree

Shirley

Shirvaun

Shivahn

Shona

Shonagh

Shonah

Shonda

Shoney

Shonta

Shontal

Shontalle

Shontelle

Shoshana

Shovonne

Shreya

Shriya

Shuna

Shunagh

Shuree

Shyla

Shynelle

Shyvonne

Sia

Sian

Siana

Siandrah

Siani

Siania

Sianna

Siany

Siara

Sibylle

Sicili

Sidaine

Sidney

Sidonie

Sidony	Sioban
Siena	Siobhan
Sienna	Siobhán
Sierra	Siobhian
Sigourney	Siofra
Sile	Síofra
Sileas	Síomha
Silíní	Siona
Silke	Sioned
Silver	Sionet
Silvia	Sionnach
Silvie	Sirena
Silvine	Siriol
Sima	Siseel
Simone	Sisely
Simonette	Siselya
Simran	Sisile
Sina	Sisiliya
Sine	Sissela
Sinead	Sissie
Sinéad	Sissy
Siobahn	Sitara

Siusan	Solana
Sive	Solange
Siwan	Solaris
Sixtine	Soleil
Siya	Solene
Skarlett	Solstice
Skie	Sonia
Sky	Sonja
Skye	Sonnagh
Skyla	Sonora
Skylah	Sonya
Skylar	Sophia
Skyler	Sophie
Slaine	Sora
Sloan	Soraya
Sloane	Sorcha
Snowdrop	Sorrel
Sofia	Soubrette
Sofie	Sparrow
Sóifia	Spéir
Sojourner	Spencer
Sol	Sri

Stacey	Sunny
Staci	Suri
Stacie	Susan
Stacy	Susana
Star	Susane
Starla	Susanna
Stefanie	Susie
Stéfhanie	Sutton
Stella	Suzanne
Stephanie	Suzette
Stephany	Swara
Stevie	Sweeney
Stoirm	Sy
Storm	Sybille
Stormi	Sydnee
Stormy	Sydney
Struan	Sylvette
Suede	Sylvia
Suesana	Sylvianne
Suhani	Sylvie
Sulwyn	Symphony
Summer	Syvonne

Tabatha	Tami
Tabetha	Tamia
Tabitha	Tamika
Taffy	Tammie
Tahlia	Tammy
Tahlor	Tananarive
Taisce	Taney
Taisie	Tangwystl
Tala	Tania
Talaith	Tanisha
Talar	Tanvi
Tali	Tanwen
Talia	Tanya
Talie	Tara
Taliesin	Tarah
Taliessin	Tarai
Taliyah	Tarian
Talliesin	Tarot
Tallulah	Tarrah
Talya	Tartan
Tamara	Taryn
Tameka	Tasha

Tatiana	Teghan
Tatum	Tegwen
Tatyana	Teleri
Tavin	Telyn
Tawna	Temperance
Tawnee	Tempesta
Tawney	Tempeste
Tawni	Tenley
Tawnia	Teresa
Tawnie	Tereson
Tawny	Teri
Taya	Terra
Tayler	Terri
Taylor	Terrwyn
Tayvia	Tesla
Tayzie	Tesni
Teagan	Tess
Teagin	Tessa
Teasagh	Thalia
Teegan	Thea
Tegan	Theodora
Tegau	Theoren

Theresa	Tierre
Therese	Tieve
Thérèse	Tiffani
Thomasette	Tiffany
Thomasine	Tigen
Thomassia	Tigernach
Tia	Tina
Tiana	Tinley
Tianna	Tinsley
Tiara	Tirian
Tieranae	Tirien
Tierani	Tirion
Tieranie	Tirrien
Tieranni	Tirruan
Tierany	Tiryan
Tiernan	Tiryon
Tiernee	Tiúilip
Tierneigh	Toille
Tierney	Toinette
Tiernie	Toinon
Tierny	Tomasa
Tierra	Toni

Tonia	Trevor
Tonya	Triage
Topaz	Tricha
Tori	Tricia
Torin	Trina
Torra	Trinity
Torrin	Trinna
Tracee	Tríonóide
Tracey	Trisha
Traci	Trista
Tracie	Tristam
Tracy	Tristan
Trahel	Tristana
Trasey	Trócaire
Trea	Trysha
Treasa	Tu
Treasey	Tulip
Treasure	Tully
Trelane	Tumajina
Tremayne	Turas
Treva	Turlough
Trevina	Turquoise

Twyla	Ursula
Tygan	Uther
Tygon	Uxia
Tyler	Vada
Tynan	Valencia
Typhaine	Valentina
Tyra	Valentine
Tyran	Valera
Tyree	Valeraine
Tyrona	Valeria
Uaine	Valerie
Uan	Valérie
Udela	Valery
Udele	Valkyrie
Ula	Vanellope
Ulani	Vanessa
Ulva	Vania
Uma	Vanille
Una	Vanitee
Unique	Vanity
Unus	Vanna
Urbain	Vannora

Vanora	Vere
Vanya	Verenice
Varda	Vériane
Vardar	Verity
Varena	Vermont
Vayda	Verone
Veda	Veronica
Vedette	Veronique
Vega	Véronique
Veira	Vevina
Velour	Vianey
Velouté	Vianna
Venice	Vianne
Venise	Vianney
Venus	Vicki
Ver	Vickie
Vera	Vicky
Véra	Victoire
Vérane	Victoria
Verania	Victorin
Veranina	Victorine
Verbena	Victrice

Vida	Vivian
Vienna	Viviana
Vignette	Viviane
Viktoria	Vivianna
Ville	Vivianne
Villette	Vivien
Vincence	Vivienne
Vincentine	Viviette
Vinciane	Vogue
Viola	Vrai
Viole	Vreni
Violet	Vyolette
Violeta	Wanda
Violett	Waverly
Violetta	Wednesday
Violette	Wendee
Viona	Wendi
Vionnet	Wendie
Virginia	Wendy
Virginie	Wentliana
Viridiana	Weslyn
Viridienne	Weylyn

Whitley	Winny
Whitney	Winter
Wilhelmina	Wisconsin
Willa	Wisteria
Willamina	Wren
Willow	Wrenley
Wilma	Wyatt
Win	Wynafred
Wina	Wynifred
Winafred	Wynn
Windy	Wynne
Winefred	Wynnie
Winefride	Wynnifred
Winefried	Wynstelle
Winfreda	Wynter
Winfrieda	Wysandra
Winifred	Xanthia
Winifryd	Xaverie
Winn	Xaviere
Winne	Xavière
Winnie	Xena
Winnifred	Ximena

Ximenna	Yareli
Xiomara	Yarely
Xitlali	Yaretzi
Xitlaly	Yaretzy
Xochitl	Yaritza
Xyla	Yasmeen
Yabell	Yasmin
Yabella	Yasmine
Yabelle	Yatzil
Yachne	Yatziri
Yadira	Yazmin
Yael	Yesenia
Yaffit	Yevette
Yahaira	Ygerna
Yakira	Yi
Yamila	Yoland
Yamilet	Yolanda
Yamileth	Yolande
Yana	Yolanthe
Yaneli	Yoselin
Yanet	Yoselyn
Yara	Yovela

Ysabel	Zada
Ysabell	Zadie
Ysabella	Zahara
Ysabelle	Zahra
Ysbel	Zaidee
Ysbella	Zaina
Yseult	Zainab
Yu	Zaira
Yula	Zakelina
Yuliana	Zamira
Yulissa	Zaniyah
Yuna	Zara
Yurani	Zarah
Yuri	Zaria
Yuritzi	Zariah
Yusra	Zariyah
Yvaine	Zavrina
Yvedt	Zaya
Yvette	Zayda
Yvonne	Zayla
Zaara	Zaylee
Zacqueline	Zayna

Zaynab

Zayra

Zeina

Zelda

Zele

Zelie

Zélie

Zella

Zena

Zenaida

Zénaïde

Zendaya

Zenia

Zenna

Zenobie

Zephrine

Zephyrine

Zéphyrine

Zerline

Zhakelina

Zhaqueline

Zhavia

Zhuri

Zia

Zinnia

Zion

Zipporah

Ziva

Ziya

Zoe

Zoey

Zoie

Zola

Zooey

Zora

Zoya

Zuill

Zulema

Zuleyka

Zuri

Zyana

Zyanya

Zyla

Printed in Great Britain
by Amazon

21173138R10088